www.ingramcontent.com/pod-product-compliance
Lightning Source LLC
Chambersburg PA
CBHW031531210526
45463CB00010B/3091

Feel the emotions of living the life you desire

What if...

Glorious new unimaginable possibilities became reality because of what you do and think today?

Attention
Intent
Emotion

What are you grateful for? How does gratitude fit into your life picture?

Today

 Ask, doodle, or draw what you want.
Then let it go and trust.

Notes

What if...

You were even more invested in this vision than you think you are right now?

We like things to manifest right away, and they may not. Many times, we're just planting a seed ...what we see in front of us might not be the end of the story.
- Sharon Salzberg

How can you build your visions into your daily life?
What does that look like?

Tomorrow

 One thing I can do tomorrow to get closer to making my vision reality:

What if...

Finances didn't dictate decisions?

Life is about, every single day, getting up to manifest your truth.
— Cory Booker

What rituals can you envision that support the future you deserve?

1 year from now

 The most urgent changes I want to make:

What if...

The possibilities were endless?

I think we manifest the very thing we put out. If you're putting out negativity, then you're going to retrieve that same sentiment. If you emanate joy, it comes back to you.
— Robin Wright

Who are some people you can share your intentions with?

5 years from now

 My visions about family, friends, work:

What if...

Things were even better than this?

Never let life impede on
your ability to manifest
your dreams.
- Corin Nemec

What are some mantras that would align with your vision?

10 years from now

 This is how I see myself and my world:

Use this journal in any way you see fit. The hope is that it brings clarity to what you really want in life, and is a springboard for your massive success!

Included in the following pages you will find places to draw and doodle your dreams for the future, inspiring quotes, and some thought provoking questions.

Have fun, and Dream Big!

*Never underestimate the
power of coffee
and a girl with a dream...*